I JUST WENT OUT TO BUY BREAD AND MILK

This is my story

Roger Clifford

Roger Clifford

Copyright © 2020 Roger Clifford

All rights reserved

No part of this book may be reproduced, or stored in a retrieval system, or transmitted in any form or by any means, electronic, mechanical, photocopying, recording, or otherwise, without express written permission of the publisher.

Cover design by: © Fizzers
Logo: ® Scottish Cartoon Art Studio

Printed in the United Kingdom
Produced for Kindle: Beech Editorial Services

ISBN: 9798646831515

CONTENTS

Title Page	1
Copyright	2
Introduction	5
America	9
Bula Vinaka – Welcome to Fiji	34
Kia Ora – Welcome to New Zealand	36
Australia: Roger the Dodger Down Under	47
Thailand	63
Singapore	73
Malaysia	75
Singapore – Dubai – London – Glasgow	77
Proceeds from my book	78
Acknowledgement	79
About The Author	85

INTRODUCTION

An Unusual Adventure Story

I had taken early retirement as a teacher a few years ago, but was still working as a supply drama teacher, employed by the local community (Glasgow City Council). Basically, I could pick up the phone whenever I wanted work and would be slotted into a school looking for a teacher. I had been thinking about travelling for quite a while and very early one morning, whilst out shopping for bread and milk, I decided to just pack some things into a rucksack, get a flight and head off. I left Glasgow, and by late afternoon, I had arrived at John F. Kennedy Airport in New York, where I was greeted by my niece and her little boy. This was where my adventure takes off. Little did I realise that I would walk through numerous cities in seven countries, cross three continents and wear out one pair of Hi-Tec trainers before I would see Scotland again. I must add that I did go through quite a few pens, pencils and notepads, and took thousands of photos on my mobile phone. I lived like a pirate, travelling across some beautiful countries and meeting beautiful people. I started posting my stories and photos on Facebook – Call yersel a Bankie and my own page, Teacher, Actor & Entrepreneur. Little did I know the number of people who would follow my travels, so I have decided to pull together my stories for friends old and new to follow my adventures – 'I only went out for bread and milk'. This is my story.

All monies from this book will go to homeless centres in Glasgow and other major cities around the world.

An Unusual Adventure Story

I had taken early retirement as a teacher a few years ago, but was still working as a supply drama teacher, employed by the local community (Glasgow City Council). Basically, I could pick up the phone whenever I wanted work and would be slotted into a school looking for a teacher.

I had been thinking about travelling for quite a while and very early one morning, whilst out shopping for bread and milk, I decided to just pack some things into a rucksack, get a flight and head off.

I left Glasgow, and by late afternoon, I had arrived at John F. Kennedy Airport in New York, where I was greeted by my niece and her little boy. This was where my adventure takes off. Little did I realise that I would walk through numerous cities in seven countries, cross three continents and wear out one pair of Hi-Tec trainers before I would see Scotland again. I must add that I did go through quite a few pens, pencils and notepads, and took thousands of photos on my mobile phone.

I lived like a pirate, travelling across some beautiful countries and meeting beautiful people.

I started posting my stories and photos on Facebook – *Call yersel a Bankie* and my own page, *Teacher, Actor & Entrepreneur*. Little did I know the number of people who would follow my travels, so I have decided to pull together my stories for friends old and new to follow my adventures – '*I only went out for bread and milk*'.

This is my story.

AMERICA

The Big Apple

Since my arrival in New York at the start of July 2018, there's been sweltering heat, nothing like I'm used to back in Clydebank (Bankieland), Scotland.

Being a tourist, I dug out my best clobber, so in my shorts, vest and hat, I left my niece's home in Maspeth, Queens and made my way to the Big Apple.

The Big Apple got its nickname from a sportswriter in the Morning Telegraph in the 1920s. He used it in his racing column *Around the Big Apple* and then musicians took it up, saying they were 'playing in the Big Apple.'

First thing I did was to make my way along 42nd St., named after the famous musical (ha, ha), and there it was, hitting me right in the kisser – Times Square. There were millions and trillions of people there! Well, I might be exaggerating a little bit, but there were an awful lot of people there. I looked all round. Every building in the square is lit up with massive advertising screens over 200 feet tall. It would take someone like Donald, 'where's your troosers', Trump to pay the electricity bills, though maybe he taps it off the White House.

But Times Square really is the ultimate symbol of New York. The crowds, the blaring horns, the towering advertising, the blaze of neon lights. As a first-time visitor, you kinda feel that there is something quite incredible at work here.

As a wee aside, Times Square was originally called Longacre Square, but this monumental crossroads had its name changed in 1904 when the *New York Times* moved its headquarters to One Times Square. The giant publishing company put on a fireworks' display on New Year's Eve and this tradition has continued ever since.

Times Square is also the world's premier showcase for theatre and film, attracting over two million people a year to its star-studded premiers.

New York City can be fun, but with the high city temperatures, it can also sap the strength right out of you. It felt like a burning inferno to me, so I was careful to have regular sit-downs. Now, I'm not one for swanky restaurants or downtown Café Bacteria, so I would find myself a humble park bench. There I would feast on my super soft mashed cheese and tomato sandwiches, gulped down with slugs from a bottle of orange juice (or OJ, as they like to call it stateside).

I started a slow shoe shuffle along 49th St., and you know what, I found myself on the famous 5th Ave. That said, most New York streets are famous for something. Anyway, I wandered down 5th Ave, and there, amongst the towering office blocks and opposite the Rockefeller Centre was Heaven, bang in the middle of the inferno. Okay, so maybe not literally Heaven, but certainly close to it. Here was the Gothic grandeur that is St. Patrick's Cathedral, spiritual home to approximately 30% of New York's Catholics.

And well, if I thought the outside was impressive, going through the large bronze doorways took my breath away. It could only be described as magical. The cavernous size is truly remarkable. It has twenty-one altars, each one dedicated to a different saint and at the top of the cathedral is a huge raised altar, made from the finest Italian marble. There is a massive organ gallery, and from here came angelic sounds (think *Phantom of the Opera* without Michael Crawford). But one thing that really struck me in this magnificent masterpiece of a building, were with number of men in dark suits protecting it. They looked like secret service agents, used to protecting the President or Beyoncé, but here they were, protecting New York's parish church (as it is affectionately known).

I stood mesmerised for a wee while in this air-conditioned Heaven on Earth and then said a little prayer for all the people who might benefit from it – friends suffering from illnesses and ailments, and not forgetting the people of Clydebank, who would no doubt need a little spiritual help to get through the Scottish summer.

Then, it was time to leg it back to Queens. Being a bit of a smart ass, I thought that I knew my way back on the subway. Aye, you guessed it, I took the wrong bloody train and added over an hour to what should have been a thirty-minute journey.

Another Day Another Dollar

I decided today that I would take a stroll around some of the wealthiest areas in the Big Apple, so headed to Madison Avenue, then Park Avenue, both on the upper east side of New York. Some of the most famous and expensive companies are situated here, and you would need more money than I had in my wallet to shop here.

I was told by my niece, who lives in New York, that a 3 apartment in one of the suburbs around New York could set you back in the excess of half a million dollars.

That's nothing; a modest penthouse apartment in New York City could cost you close to 50 million big ones. Yip you heard right… Phew!!! You would need to have a fancy surname like Beckham to own one of these gold wallpaper penthouses, which the Beckham's do, along with a penthouse in Miami valued at over 50 million sweet ones.

Some of the wealthiest people in the planet live on Madison and Park (not many teachers, I should think) and it's here that you will also find the famous Waldorf Astoria Hotel. This is one of the most expensive and luxurious hotels in New York. If you like watching movies, it has featured in many of them including *Maid in Manhattan, Hannah and Her Sisters* and the *Godfather III,* and not forgetting *Week-end at the Waldorf,* for those fans of films from the 1940s.

I spotted quite a few differences between here and the west of Scotland, and one of the things I noticed, as I looked up at the skyscrapers, was that there was not one piece of washing hanging out anywhere. My mum would have been shocked that no one was making the best of the good drying day, but it did make these concrete giants look so clean in the glistening sun. Okay, so I bet you're wondering why nobody hangs out their washing, not even a pair of socks or knickers. Well, I'll tell you, you'll get fined if you do, making it more expensive than turning on the tumble drier.

I'll tell you a funny story about what happened to me on Madison Ave. As I said, I was in my sartorial best vest and two-pound shorts, casually walking down the avenue, taking photos, but with my laptop under my arm. It suddenly occurred to me, that this might not be the most sensible thing to do (trusting Scot, as I am, expecting to be mugged at any moment). Anyway, Madison Ave, or not, I saw a Ralph Lauren plastic bag that looked like it would be the right size to conceal my laptop. Okay, so it was sticking out of a bin, so let's call it reusing.

The thing was, I kept wondering why I was getting smiles (and the occasional strange look) from people walking by. Then I realised, maybe they were thinking 'That guy, with the crazy designer shorts on, must have bought his girl something nice in Ralph Lauren. Lucky girl.' I just smiled back.

Pretty Woman Walking Down the Street

A day out at the theatre is always a day to treasure, and so I went to the Netherlander Theatre on 41st St. to see *Pretty Woman*. The theatre has over 1200 seats and is conveniently tucked away between 7th and 8th Avenue.

This was three hours of bliss in the middle of the Concrete Jungle. Fantastic, superb, exhilarating, exciting, wonderful. The show had great performances along with amazing visual effects and fantastic choreography. A far cry from my own past performances in pantomimes like *Jack the Lad* and *Mother Goose* at Glasgow's Mitchell Theatre, let alone the smaller venues and town halls.

New York, New York, So Good They Named It Twice

Today's stroll took me along 42nd Street, and Broadway. As usual it was warm, okay, so it was roasting hot, but luckily there are lots of parks dotted throughout New York offering some shade.

The first park of the day was Bryant Park which was full of holiday-makers and office workers, out enjoying their lunch break. I lay for a while, spread eagled, on the grass, in the warm sun. We were entertained by a couple of American boy bands, treating the audience to their own brand of music. I liked their music, and would have enjoyed more of it if I was here with friends, enjoying a wine or, better still, an ice-cold beer, in the heat of the day. But it was time to move on.

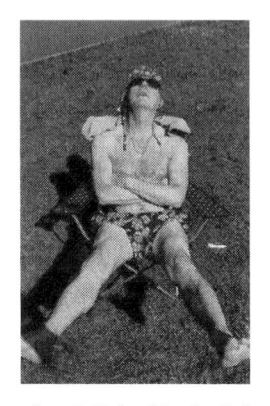

I made my way back up through Times Square and into Central Park. If you fancy a stroll around Central Park, I have some advice, get yourself fit, there's a lot of ground to cover. There are street entertainers wherever you go in the park, and having done some acting myself, I have to say, I love all the razzmatazz.

Roger the Dodger falls asleep in the sun

For theatre lovers, there is the Delacorte Theater, an outdoor arena created by the New York publisher and philanthropist, George T Delacorte. The theatre is home to the world-famous Shakespeare in the Park which is free (if you don't mind spending time queueing for tickets).

There is also a zoo in the park, which gives you an idea of how big the park is (it's 843 acres, for those of you who like facts), and it's a great place for families to go to escape the urban jungle. It really is a great place to forget you are in one of the busiest cities in the world. Most tranquil of all, is the Loch in the Ravine/North Woods section of the park. It is absolutely beautiful. It did bring memories of my own favourite Scottish loch: Loch Ness, home to Nessie, the famous monster. Only my loch is of a much larger and grander scale. If you would like to go out for a relaxing time on the water in the Ravine/North Woods, you can hire rowing boats. You would be a brave person to go out in a rowing boat in Scotland's Loch Ness, cause Nessie the monster might just get ya.

You could spend a whole holiday exploring the sites in the park – the Wollman Rink (maybe not for high summer, but perfect when the temperature drops); Strawberry Fields (built in memory of

John Lennon); Belvedere Castle (the perfect spot for a proposal – quick run); and the more sombre, though no less beautiful Bethesda Fountain, which commemorates those who died in the Civil War.

One of the most exciting things I saw while wandering around the park, was a production crew, filming scenes for a new TV series called *Instinct* starring fellow Scot, Alan Cumming. I don't know Alan personally, but we both studied at the Royal Scottish Academy of Music and Drama (now the Royal Conservatoire of Scotland, if you please). Apparently, the series is about murders in Central Park and wider Manhattan I never got to see the series, but if there are repeats, I'll have a quiet laugh to myself knowing that I was there.

No need to worry about murder, though, as there are plenty of park rangers driving around in their Jeeps and NYPD cars too, driving slowly, lights flashing, ready to question anyone they think might be able to 'help them with their inquiries'.

My favoured mode of transport in the park was Shanks's pony (i.e. my own two feet), but if you prefer, you can travel by horse and carriage, bike, boat or skateboard. Run, jog, walk, whatever you like, but for me, it was time to make my way out of the park.

On my way through the streets to the subway, I was entertained by more street performers, and even on-board the train, I enjoyed a session from a few musicians who jammed for their fellow passengers, making their weary way back home.

Family Ties

My grandfather also named Roger Clifford, arrived in New York with his younger brother, Michael Clifford on the 7th of April 1913. They had been travelling on the ship Franconia, from Liverpool, England.

They were met on the quayside by another brother William

Clifford, who welcomed them to America.

Very shortly afterwards William sent for his love in Ireland Delia Kenny to join him in New York, the land of opportunity.

Now, this is where the story gets good. On the day that Delia, arrived in New York, William couldn't get away from his work,, and so he sent my grandfather Roger Clifford to collect her at the quayside. So the story goes...They only had eyes for each other...Mmmm Ohh.

Shortly afterwards my grandfather's brother and his fiancé Delia, broke up their relationship. My grand pappy then asked his brother if he could date Delia, which his brother agreed to. And why not? Their relationship had broken up.

Within a short period of time, my grandfather and Delia, who was to be my grandmother, married and moved from the Bronx to Manhattan.

My grandfather started work as a driver on the New York trains, while Delia, worked in hospitals and nurseries, as a nurse and midwife.

Unfortunately, one day a young man committed suicide by throwing himself in front of the train, my grandfather was driving. My grandfather came off his train, and never drove one again.

My own father, Roger (yes, we do like to keep the name in the family, as my son's name is also Roger) was born in New York, as was his brother and one sister.

Then unlike most Irish families, who left Ireland during the famine never to return, my grandfather, grandmother, with their two sons and one daughter, arrived back in Ireland, where land was plentiful. My father was by then 12 years of age. Back in Ireland my grandparents had four more daughters and lived a happy, contented and loving life.

Now that's a love story....

We're Going to Need a Bigger Boat – Long Island

When the temperature in New York was pushing into the 90s, this Bankie decided it was time to get a breath of fresh air, so headed to Long Beach. The resort was founded here around 1880, which makes it even older than me, though some might disagree. The first hotel was quickly followed by the railroad, bringing New Yorkers here for their holidays, or as they would say, vacation.

The beach itself is over three miles long and has a boardwalk along the pier, stretching nearly two miles, which can be easier on the feet than treading sand.

Property in Long Island is expensive, but I found the prices were right when I sat down for a meal and a drink.

Don't get too comfortable though, as this place is also famous for sharks, especially of the Great White variety. The beach even has its own celebrity shark called Mary-Lee. She was first caught a few years ago and was tagged to allow for research into her habits. At that time, she weighed in at 3,490lbs and was 16ft in length. She's visited three times in the last three years, so you might be un/lucky enough to catch a glimpse.

The local radio station announces when Mary-Lee is going to make an appearance as her tag sends satellite readings, so her location can be pinpointed. It's been calculated that she has travelled over 34,000 miles in the last three years, coming in from the deep ocean to give birth each year to more Great Whites.

Thankfully, there are lifeguards all along the stretch of water, keeping a close eye on everyone, and ensuring that no one goes too far out and into dangerous waters.

To keep you cool, there are plenty of facilities along the beach and a nice breeze, which makes Scottish skin burn even faster.

We're all Going to a Tea Party

One of the things I was really interested in was to find out about the history of Boston, so I followed the Boston Freedom Trail. The trail is around two and a half miles long and is marked by a trail of red bricks set into the pavement, going from Boston Common to the Bunker Hill Monument in Charlestown.

There are loads of points of interest along the way, some Colonial and some Federal. The trail takes in the principle chapters of the people, places and events that sparked the American Revolution, the fight for freedom against the British. It also highlights the role Boston was to play in the foundations of the new nation.

After the trail, I took in a highly entertaining family show at Boston Harbour – The Boston Tea Party. The history behind the Tea Party is that in December 1773, the natives of Boston (Colonists), tired of British taxes, stormed aboard one of the British ships and threw hundreds of chests of tea into the harbour. It was said that the place smelt of tea for weeks after the event, though the heat made me reach for another ice cream, rather than a pot of tea.

Lady Liberty and Ellis Island

After returning from Boston, I had one of the most interesting and enjoyable days since I had started my trip. I had an early start from Queens, taking the train to South Ferry station where I took the boat to see the great lady herself. I must admit to feeling a little apprehensive, hoping I wouldn't be disappointed by this great marvel.

Even before it took its place at the gateway to America, the Statue of Liberty overwhelmed those who saw it.

It started life as an idea from a group of Parisian intellectuals led by Edouard de Laboulaye. They were fighting against political oppression in France but decided to honour the ideals of freedom with a symbolic gift to the United States (that's quite some gift). The time was right for such a gesture. The Civil War was over. Slavery had been abolished and the nation looked forward to its centennial anniversary.

The statue was sculpted by Frederic Auguste Bartholdi, with metal framework by a certain Monsieur Eiffel, and it was constructed in Paris in the 1880s. At the time this colossus was proclaimed: 'The Eighth Wonder of the World'.

Lady Liberty is based on a likeness of a Roman goddess and the inscription on the tablet she holds gives the date in roman numerals of the US Declaration of Independence.

When she was moved onto her pedestal in 1886, not only was she the tallest structure in New York City, but also the tallest statue in the world.

I must admit that the trip was well-worth the cost. It was a great day out, mixing with hundreds of different nationalities, all capturing photos of themselves at this iconic place.

Then it was on to Ellis Island. Millions of people all over the world have some connection with ancestors who came through Ellis Island. Whether from religious persecution, political strife, unemployment or lured by the adventure, these were the circumstances of the greatest migration in modern history, when shipload after shipload brought people from Europe to the United States.

Most took their first steps on American soil on Ellis Island, and today it is a memorial to those who made this nation their home. It is reckoned that between 1886 and 1924, over fourteen million immigrants entered America through New York.

There is also an amazing archive on the island, where you can look up family records to trace relatives who immigrated in the past. I knew a little about my background, so I decided to check out the Ellis Island Immigration Library. I discovered that my grandfather, also Roger Clifford, arrived in New York in 1913 on a boat from Liverpool. He met my grandmother Delia, who had been in New York from before my grandfather arrived there. She was on the quayside with her fiancé, my grandfather's brother, on the quayside. But when they broke up, my grandparents got together and married in New York. My grandfather became a train driver in the city and my grandmother became a nurse in hospitals in the Big Apple. Most of this story has been told in my grandfather and grandmother's love story earlier in Family Ties, New York

My father, same name again, Roger Clifford, was born in Manhattan and lived there until he was 12 years old. Even though he left America when he was 12 years old, he never really spoke with an American accent, but did use the word 'yea', instead of yes. Then his family moved back to Ireland, but the lack of work brought my parents over to Clydebank, Glasgow where there was an abundance of opportunities in the period after the war, and that is where my sister and I were born and brought up.

Mr Clifford Goes to Washington

I decided to venture a bit further in my travels in the U.S and set off from New York to Washington. Memories went back to a few years earlier when I was teaching at a very large secondary school in Glasgow. I had the opportunity to take part in a teacher exchange programme. I was going to teach at a high school in North Carolina, and another teacher from North Carolina would come to my school in Glasgow. I was to be stationed in Washington for a week prior to joining my new high school as an introduction. The aim of the programme was to highlight different teaching methods and values within our different countries and backgrounds. I was ready for the exchange when the other teacher, for personal reasons, had to pull out. I was tempted to take a bus ride from Washington to North Carolina, just to see the high school where I would have been teaching years before. But considering it was nearly 300 miles, I quickly discounted the idea and just headed into Washington as I planned to explore this wonderful city.

My first stop, which might sound a bit morbid, was to visit Arlington Cemetery. But let me explain, as a child of the 60s, I grew up with the unsolved mystery of JFK's assassination, so I knew that I had to visit his grave at Arlington.

There's a hop-on-hop-off trolley bus that takes you round the cemetery, going slowly enough for people to take photos while listening to the driver's commentary about the history of this place and the famous people buried here.

I stopped at the grave of John F. Kennedy, where he is buried with his wife, First Lady Jacqueline Kennedy Onassis. There's an eternal flame burning above the President's grave, though it has apparently gone out twice since it was lit. The first occasion was in 1963 when a group of Catholic school kids threw some holy water on the grave and extinguished the flame by mistake.

The Washington Gas Company decided that they should come up with a better system and now there is a constantly igniting spark which keeps the flame alight, no matter the weather.

If one assassinated president wasn't enough, next I took a walk to the Lincoln monument. In theory, it wasn't a long walk, but with a rucksack, laptop, litres of water and 90 degree heat, I felt every step.

The memorial was built in honour of the 16th president of the United States. The statue of Lincoln is really impressive and is housed in a building based on an ancient Greek temple. The statue itself is made from Georgian white marble and is 19 feet tall (though it was originally only going to be 10 feet tall). Luckily though, they didn't do him standing, as at 28 feet, his head would be through the roof.

On the other side of the National Mall is the Washington Monument, built as a memorial for the first president of the United States. The monument is very impressive standing proud above a reflecting pool. At the time it was built, it became the tallest structure in the world (at 555 feet), although it held the title for only five years, when the Eiffel Tower took over the honours.

The area was packed with all nationalities, with loads of children running around enjoying some freedom, and lots of ice lollies and ice cream. The vendors seemed particularly happy, although I would be too if I was taking in a small fortune every day.

On the way back to my lodgings, after a day of contemplation, I passed a gospel church. The service must have just finished, as the congregation spilled onto the pavement, still singing, with rhythm in their souls. I loved the atmosphere as it surrounded me. I could have danced along the pavements, if I was encouraged.

Streets of Philadelphia

Time to leave Washington, and after a journey along a jam-packed motorway and a quick stop in Baltimore, I made it to Philadelphia.

It was late in the evening when I arrived, and my stomach told me it would be a good time to seek out Chinatown. The restaurants were packed, which is always a good sign, and the food was really good value for money. It was getting dark though, so I didn't linger, but bought some spicy noodles and a bottle of water to take away. I was glad I bought the water, because the noodles were the spiciest I'd ever eaten. I swear I was breathing fire out of my nostrils like some dragon from Game of Thrones.

My day's travel and burning mouth made me decide to head for my accommodation and while I made it to the underground station near my digs, there was a bit of an anxious moment as I came out of the underground. There was a group of youths at the top of the stairs, and they were beginning to fight. I thought quickly with my good old Scottish brain, an American might have said 'I'll hail a fast car', but for me it was, 'I'm getting my arse out of here.' Phew, made it to my digs and before long, it was beddy bye byes time.

The next morning, I decided to brave the big city again, and had a great time wandering about. Just to let you know, you might think that one big city looks pretty much like another, but you do see the differences, especially away from the centre. There are modestly well-to-do people, smartly dressed and walking about with purpose, then there are others who obviously have seen a rougher side of life. There was one guy pushing a shopping trolley around with him. Something that your granny used to use when she went shopping, which was overflowing with plastic bags. It looked like he had everything he owned in that trolley. I really do feel for people like that. I've tried to help out in Scotland, and promised myself that I would do so again, when I got home.

I had often heard about the Liberty Bell, and here I was, in the beautiful city of Philadelphia, with a chance to see it. It is not just a work of art; it also played an important role in American history.

Now, have you ever looked at a queue and wondered if it was worth joining? Well, this queue went around the square of 6th St and into Market St. I really thought that nothing was worth waiting that long for, but in spite of myself, I joined the queue and boy was I glad.

The Liberty Bell is a huge bronze bell which has come to symbolise freedom. It sits in Independence Hall, and if you ever get a chance to see it, I would highly recommend you do. Okay, so it's got a big crack on it, but that makes it more interesting. In fact, it was supposed have cracked on two occasions. No one is quite sure how the bell got its first crack. One theory is that it happened when it was tested on its arrival in Philadelphia, in 1752. The second time it cracked was supposedly in February 1846, when it was rung on Presidents Day. Nonetheless, it was rung to celebrate the first public reading of the Declaration of Independence, so is very dear to the American people, so dear in fact, that early souvenir hunters chipped off bits of it.

If You Are Going to San Francisco...

Whenever I arrive in a new city, I always want to find out a little about the place. I read that San Francisco was a gold rush town. The stampede started in 1849 and would lead to prosperity for some, heartache for others, but ultimately a good name for their American football team – the 49ers.

San Francisco is a really vibrant city, but it has had its fair share of tragedies. A huge earthquake hit in 1906, where approximately

3,000 people died, and fires ravaged the city.

Another earthquake hit in 1989, where there were over 60 reported deaths. Luckily the devastation shown in the Rock's action movie *San Andreas* hasn't come to pass, and San Fran has risen from the dust.

It did have another tragedy to deal with though. During the 1960s and 70s, the infamous Zodiac killer terrorised the city. In a letter he sent, goading the police, he confessed to no less than 37 murders, though they could confirm only five. The murderer has never been caught and it remains one of America's unsolved cases.

Enough dark shadows, San Francisco shines brightly in the sun or it does when the fog doesn't obscure the view. But it really is one of the most beautiful cities in the world. There's lots of things to see and do – Van Ness, the Theater and Garden Districts and Golden Gate Park (home to California's Academy of Sciences).

Then there is Haight Asbury, the birthplace of the 1960s' historic vibe, which still sells everything a hippy could, want from vintage clothing to records and books. I remember myself back in the late 1970s when the trend and my style was a little bit hippy. I used to wear bellbottom trousers which were tight at the arse and upper leg, but then bellowed out at the bottom. I wore a sleeveless, multi-coloured tank top and had long hair. But the most amazing thing was that I wore dark patent shiny shoes, which had anything from 6 to 8-inch platforms. They looked the business, but I could hardly walk in them. Many a time after a couple of drinks, my girlfriend had to take my arm to help me along the road, and I'm no kiddin.

I have been to many places throughout the world on travels, but I don't think I've ever been to more hilly streets, than San Francisco. You need to be fit, if you intend walking around Frisco. Bradford Street was the steepest street that I've ever walked.

When I got to the top, my legs were like Long John Silver's wooden peg, except times two.

While Haight Ashbury might not be the place to visit with kids, Pier 39 and Fisherman's Wharf is a great place to take a stroll. It's a really busy tourist attraction with lots of entertainment, bars, restaurants and great live music. But you don't need to confine yourself to this area, as there are great places to eat all over the city, particularly in Chinatown and Japanese Town.

One thing I was really keen to do was see the Golden Gate Bridge. The bridge was constructed between 1933 and 1937 and became one of the world's most iconic structures. Sceptics doubted that the feat of spanning San Francisco Bay could be done. But hey, they managed, and I walked the mile across it and, why not, the mile back too. Windy, very windy, but great fun.

I also wanted to see the Giants' Baseball Ground. Not only was the vast stadium really impressive, but I also got a view of the harbour with millionaires' boats anchored alongside the stadium. It made me laugh, quite different from stadiums of Scotland's two big teams – Celtic and Rangers. The police would need to employ frogmen to fish out their supporters if they got into a brawl.

Then it was on to Pacific Heights, recently named the most expensive neighbourhood in the United States. As you can imagine, it is a rather desirable area, but with starting prices around $2 million dollars, you would need more than desire to move here. If you're lucky to have a job, you would need a lot of overtime to pay the mortgage.

Silicon Valley is another really desirable area in San Francisco. It is the global centre for the high-tech industry, and again, you've got to be very rich to live here. I did visit though and had dinner with an old friend and his family. The houses here are out of this world, but I would see more during my time in America, when I moved on to Beverley Hills.

Slightly less desirable is Alcatraz. For hundreds of years this lonely island in the Bay only had occasional visitors in the form of the Milwauk Native Americans, but it was largely unused.

That was until it was used as a military prison between 1859 and 1933, before becoming a Federal Penitentiary from 1934 to 1963. The island and prison have been the subject of many films and books over the years (including *The Rock, Escape from Alcatraz* and *Birdman of Alcatraz,* which was based on a real prisoner who tamed birds to keep him company). Other notorious inmates included some of America's most violent – Al Capone and Machine Gun Kelly to name just two.

The island is now in decay, but I don't know how anyone could have survived this hell hole. I found it really eerie, as though there was still a mysterious presence about it.

Although there were never any executions on Alcatraz, there were five suicides, eight murders and a handful of would-be escapees were shot. The authorities said that no one every escaped, although there were some who made it as far as the water and were 'missing presumed drowned.' With escape, not an option, inmates had to wait until the authorities thought they were safe enough to be released back into society. I know, don't laugh.

I mentioned Machine Gun Kelly before, well the man who riddled everyone and everything with holes before he was imprisoned, ended up being an altar boy to the prison chaplain. Had the Penitentiary reformed him? Mmm.

Society has found a more pleasant use for the island though and it is now home to a bird sanctuary, just a quarter of a mile from all the sights and sounds of the beautiful city of San Francisco.

Los Angeles - I'm Ready for My Close-Up, Mr Clifford

Since I was a you boy, I loved watching American films, and nothing said America more to me than a Greyhound bus. Now, at long last, I had my chance, so I boarded the Greyhound, left San Francisco and headed south to Los Angeles. The journey took about seven hours and wasn't as comfortable as I thought it would be. I was sitting next to a rather overweight lady, who took up not only her own seat, but part of mine as well. In her arms she had a bag, which looked like it contained her full wardrobe, which didn't help the matter one little bit.

After a long journey through California, taking in San Jose (*Do you know the way, to San Jose?*) and San Fernando (that's another famous song). My, they sure like their saints here, I reached LA., or as some would have it, the City of Angels (more heavenly creatures). As usual the weather was toasting, but here I was at last, in the home of some of the biggest TV and movie production companies – like Paramount, Universal and Warner Brothers.

Los Angeles is a massive city, so I decided there was no better place to start than Hollywood, specifically Hollywood Boulevard. The Boulevard's sidewalk is embedded with over 2,500 brass stars bearing the names of some of the world's most famous film stars. I was always a fan of the actor Dustin Hoffman, who acted in great films like *The Graduate* and *Midnight Cowboy*, to mention a few. I did get chatting to this guy one night who was walking his dog along this famous sidewalk. At a glance I thought, *Is that Hoffman, the famous Dustin Hoffman*, but I'm afraid it wasn't. But I'll tell you, it did look very like him. Maybe on my return home I should go to Specsavers.

While the star trail travels along 15 blocks, it wasn't as impressive as I had imagined. It does have the bright lights, but mainly it's just full of tourists sitting on the pavement, taking photos of their favourite stars' names. The shops that line the street aren't glamourous either but are just full of souvenirs.

I suppose the tourists give a certain atmosphere to the place, but there is a downside to the place too. Drugs are a big part of life here, and it being Hollywood, everything seems more dramatic. There are buskers on the streets, but the bigger performances come from the drug-crazed nutters who argue with cars going by, and chase after them. Maybe not the best place to take children at night.

One of the things that I did admire was the beautiful Roosevelt Hotel, named after the 26th president, on Hollywood Boulevard. It's really elegant and looks majestic when lit up at night.

Next to conquer was the famous Hollywood sign on Mount Lee, part of the Santa Monica Mountains. Most people use four wheels to get as near to the sign as possible, but I'm not most people. Guess what? I hiked it – from Hollywood Boulevard, I climbed and I climbed and then I climbed some more, up the steep hill, which turned into a steep mountain.

I did feel really proud of myself when I reached the top, especially as I passed a lot of younger guys who were completely breathless. I kept going and got all the photos and selfies that I wanted.

As a solo traveller and knowing that I couldn't see everything in the cities I visited, I concentrated on what would make me happy. And so, after a short subway ride, I arrived at Universal Studios and Theme Park. Now, this really should be on everyone's bucket list. There are so many things to do, it would take you the whole day to complete. Some of the big attractions are: The Wizarding World of Harry Potter and the Jurassic World ride. There's fun here for all the family, but don't rush it, and remember the golden rule in the heat of the day is to eat as many ice lollies and cones as you can, to keep you from getting dehydrated of course. You will need to take plenty of money with you. Personally, I walked around through the park without going on anything.

I also loved Beverly Hills which was so far away from my normal life in Clydebank as you can imagine. But here I was, walking through Beverly Hills with my wee rucksack, passing the jet-set in their designer clothes. I did get to enjoy the mellow rhythm and blues coming out of the fancy shops though – that, you get for free.

There was also a plethora of open-fronted restaurants, and while I couldn't afford to eat in them, they seemed to be doing a roaring trade. I had a sneaky look around, and everyone looked mega-rich. I also tried to see if there was anyone famous. There was one woman with high cheek bones and extremely pouted red lips. Maybe Joan Rivers? Then again, maybe not ... I've been told that she died in 2014

Now, this is a fantastic story I'm going to tell you. You see sometimes extraordinary things can happen in the course of a person's life. Acting has played a great part in my life, for many years, and I'll never forget the times I had and will always cherish them. There was always so much fun travelling around the country performing, everywhere and anywhere. Never was there a dull moment.

Anyway, a few years ago, I had been working with a theatre company with some Glasgow actors and we were asked to perform a gig at the world-famous Glastonbury Festival. To fill in the time between the music acts on the big stages, we had to act out some light entertainment acts as comedy characters, much to the delight of the crowd.

Suddenly, Amy Winehouse, the sad to say, now deceased singer, appeared on stage to rapturous applause. Someone from the side of the stage came on with an ice bucket which had a bottle of champagne in it. Amy poured a glass and we never thought anymore of it.

But on the Sunday evening, as our company was packing up our van before we set off on the long journey north, Amy Winehouse's stage was being dismantled. Things from the stage were getting thrown into a rubbish skip. As I was passing, I looked into the skip and could see an aluminium heart-shaped ice bucket ... the one Amy had used the day before. Now, that ice bucket was far too nice to throw away, so I took it with me, all the way back home to Glasgow.

I do have actor friends to confirm this story and, on the rare occasion, when we have some guests over at the house, a nice bottle of prosecco is placed in an ice bucket chilled with lots of ice, but it's not an ordinary ice bucket, it's Amy Winehouse's ice bucket!!!

Anyway, back to America without Poor Amy who never made it passed 27, but here I was walking by a fancy shop selling anti-aging products in Beverly Hills.

'Would you like to try some beauty treatments?' A smart young man asked.

I looked around, but it seemed he was talking to me. 'I'm fae Glasgow son. And anyway, do you even know what age I am?'

He looked me up and down, then coyly said, 'Around 60.'

Cheeky bugger, 'I'm not a day over 40,' I blurted.

'Well, sir, for just $300 we could do something for your eyes. It would just take 30 minutes.'

'Why?' I asked. At that price, I'd be expecting a new pair, with perfect vision. 'What kind of eyes do you think I've got?'

'Ping-pong ball eyes, sir.' Charming.

So, I took myself away and found somewhere to eat my humble little sandwich and ponder on how lucky I was to be here, amongst the rich and famous, even with my ping-pong eyes!

Now, when I was wee, I used to watch a TV series called *77 Sunset Strip* which was set in Beverly Hills. I was really enamoured with the programme and used to ask my mum if we could move to America and live in the Hills.

'What? I'm not taking you away from your school,' she would say. 'Your teacher says you're doing well.'

Thinking about it now, I don't think that was the only reason we had for not swapping the life we had in Scotland. But here I was, on Sunset Boulevard. The houses here looked more like luxurious hotels than people's houses. The other thing that struck me was how many women I saw, driving along the Boulevard with little dogs, bows in their hair, sitting on their laps.

Now, I have to say, the women all looked fabulous, although most will have had plastic surgery along the way. As for the men? Well, not a baldy in sight. Does the sun help them keep their hair? Personally, I think they've all had transplants. So what if your birth certificate says you're 80? With the right amount of cash, you can wipe 30 years off that little kisser of yours.

Continuing my walk, I thought of some of the famous folk who live here – Jack Nicholson, Katy Perry, Eddie Murphy, Leonardo DiCaprio, Kevin Costner, to name just a few.

All people with one thing in common – they are extremely wealthy and with the money they have they could own a house in every city. Funny thing is; many of them do.

I also took a trip to the very interesting John Paul Getty Museum. Not only was Getty a successful businessman, he also loved collecting art. The owner of the Getty Oil Company once said: 'There's a personal gratification collecting art objects that have true and lasting beauty.' When he died in 1976, Getty left the bulk of his considerable fortune to the museum.

Well, that's me done in America – where to next?

BULA VINAKA – WELCOME TO FIJI

After a flight over the South Pacific, I arrive at the next stop on my adventure, the beautiful island of Fiji, with its palm lined beaches, coral reefs and crystal-clear lagoons.

I stayed close to the airport in Nadi on Fiji's main island, Viti Levu, and travelled around the place by bus. Public transport isn't too modern here, in fact, I think it's fair to say that the buses are old. You can't rely on the timetables here, either. When you ask what time the bus will come, the locals say, 'Fiji time,' which basically means, whenever.

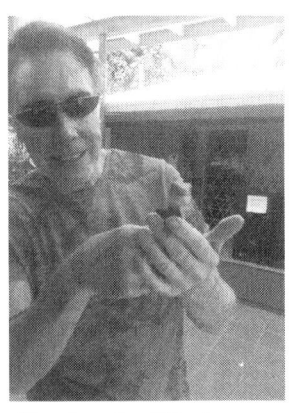

But Fiji time, means that driving around the island is relaxing, with no one in a hurry. You pass little huts (a bit of a contrast to Beverly Hills) and there's an abundance of goats and chickens running about the place. There is a lovely smell to the place, as there are always barbecues wafting sweet smoke into the air. The island is so picturesque, with amazing long beaches and scenery to die for (in fact, it might just be what Paradise looks like).

The local people here are quite poor and have to rely on everyday markets to make their living. There are so many market stalls, though, it's a wonder anyone can make much money at all. The currency here is the Fiji dollar and for a Westerner, the cost of staying here is really cheap. You feel like a millionaire when see how much your Fiji dollars can buy.

The Garden of the Sleeping Giant is one area in Nadi that is well-worth a visit. It has landscaped lawns, fountains and ponds, and the star attractions, over 40 varieties of orchid. There's a Hollywood connection here too, as the garden was once owned by Ironside himself, the actor Raymond Burr. The gardens are only four miles north of the airport but are tranquil in the extreme.

If your spirits haven't been nurtured enough by nature in Fiji, you could also visit the Hindu temple in Nadi town, which reflects the Indian origins of many who live in Fiji.

If you believe in reincarnation, you might take your chances with a Diving with the Sharks experience (I'm assured it's very safe). During the dive you can see up to eight different species of shark, including sicklefin lemons, grey reefs, massive bulls and tiger sharks.

If you prefer your adventures on dry land, then there's the Kula Wild Adventure Park. It sits on the coast near the town of Sigatoka, which is around two hours by bus from Nadi. It's advertised as a family park, but I must just be a big kid, because I loved it. It has water slides that take you through a real jungle, and there's a chance to hold iguanas and snakes and see animals native to Fiji, like the flying fox. There are also fruit bats, parrots of every colour and coral displays that take your breath away.

Sadly, that was my time over in Fiji, but given the chance, I'll definitely come back.

Moce Fiji (pronounced Mothay Fiji) Goodbye Fiji.

KIA ORA – WELCOME TO NEW ZEALAND

Auckland - Revolving Restaurants: and Free-falling Dare Devils

Auckland is the largest city in New Zealand with a population of around 1.5 million people. It has great shopping outlets, bars and restaurants, and is a very clean and vibrant place. The iconic giant in the skyline, Sky Tower, has a revolving restaurant, giving 360-degree views of the city. The restaurant is called The Orbit, and at 1,100 feet in the air, you do feel like you are in orbit, as you look down on the city below.

I was treated by my daughter, daughter-in-law and grandson, to a lovely birthday dinner there, with some wine to calm my nerves, as I watched free-fall divers leap off the tower and down the side of the building. It's awesome to watch, but only for dare devils. I had posted a few photos of these free-falling nutters back home, on social media sites … and before I knew it, I received messages back, asking if it was me free falling from the Orbit.

My message back was blunt: 'Are you kidding? Are you aff, your heid? Not only can I hardly look down from heights; I can't look up at heights either.'

I thought of my dinner in the revolving restaurant as a unique experience, little knowing that it was one that would be repeated in other places, high up in the sky, during my worldwide adventure.

While I might not have the courage to jump off a building, I did take a walk across the floor. You might not think that would take much bravery until I tell you that the floor is made of thickened glass and you can see directly down 610 feet to the ant-like people on the ground. Not everyone had the nerves to try it and it was quite amusing watching their abortive attempts at that first step. I managed, but I did feel very uneasy, what if today was the day the glass failed?

Thankfully it didn't, so I rewarded myself with a coffee as I looked out over the Viaduct harbour.

One of the most amazing places that I had a chance to visit was Muriwai Beach, which is about 45 minutes west of Auckland. The beach is most famous for its gannet colony. These migratory birds are fascinating to watch as they swoop down into the Tasman Sea below. They dive-bomb into the ocean at around 100mph, catching fish to feed themselves and their young. It's breathtaking watching them and while you do, you get a great view over the cliffs to the sea and can really appreciate the beauty of this special place.

Mission Bay is another scenic spot and is home to great fish restaurants selling fresh local products. Try the fresh prawn salad and you won't be disappointed.

With all that good food in my belly, it was time for a walk, so I made my way to Mount Wellington, an extinct volcano (fingers crossed), where you can walk around the perimeter of the crater. You also get a great view of the Auckland suburbs from the top.

A few days later, I hiked up Mount Eden, also formed by volcanic activity. It has good hiking and jogging trails and you can get a great view of the Eden Park, home to the All Blacks rugby union team.

Tauranga

Heading south, while staying on New Zealand's North Island, I visited the Mount Maunganui area of Tauranga. The area is renowned for its beaches and mountains, Maunganui rises from base to peak an impressive 230 metres, not far off 800 feet. There's a choice of tracks leading up to the summit and it gets quite steep at some points. I can assure you, it's well-worth the effort as you get fantastic views of the harbour, beach and the Pacific Ocean from the top.

The beach is ideal for surfers and if you are lucky, you might see some dolphins skimming, just below the surface of the waves, chasing away the stingrays who also make this area their home.

There's also a population of blue penguins here, who come ashore at night-time to their burrows.

After all my walking, I wanted to get more of a feeling for the culture of New Zealand, so I went to Tamaki Maori Village to experience traditional Maori life.

The singing and traditional dances were fantastic, and we were shown how to perform the Haka (made famous by the All Blacks rugby team). I was given the special honour of being made a Maori chief (so, a little respect please). My duties for the day included leading a group of tourists around the village. I was given a traditional Maori blessing from one of the chiefs which consisted of his nose and forehead gently touching my nose and forehead. I tried to repay the compliment, a little later on, during the ceremony, but instead of gently touching each other's noses and foreheads, I kind of clashed them a little too hard together. This startled the audience and frightened the chief. If you had been there, you would have thought that I was giving the big chief, the Glasgow kiss, by sticking the heid on him.

We remained friends though, and the experience ends with a show and a great dinner, which is prepared in an unusual way. The food is cooked using the power of the heat from the volcano, on the mountain side. We were told that the underground lava and hot earth cooks the food and not only does it taste delicious, but the food is enriched by vitamins and minerals. Loved it.

Rotorua

If you are looking for another fun day out, then I would highly recommend a visit to the Skyline Trail in Rotorua. You can travel uphill in a gondola cable car and come down on a luge, yes, you heard right, like in the Winter Olympics, but without the snow (at least at this time of year). Alternatively, you can ride through the forests on mountain bikes, or have a more sedate round of golf or a massage at the spa.

You'll no doubt build up an appetite with all that activity, and you're well-catered for with a lovely wee restaurant at the top of the gondola ride.

There's a buffet serving local sea food or expertly prepared meat dishes, and all at reasonable prices. While you're there, you might as well top it all off with a large helping of delicious ice cream. Yum, what a day.

Waipu – Bream Bay

If you ever come to New Zealand and have some Scottish blood flowing through your veins, you might enjoy a trip to Waipu in the Whangarei district. Situated at the northern tip of the North Island, Waipu has a long connection with Scotland. In the 1800s, many Highland Scots left the poverty and stark living conditions behind and became the first Western settlers in this area. Rather than be viewed with suspicion, the Maori people welcomed them. The men were skilled in carpentry, building and making things. While the women were excellent nurses and kept the place clean, tidy and presentable to travellers who were passing through. The Maori welcomed the Scots with open arms and many friendships and marriages were formed between the two communities.

Some Scots chose not to settle there, but continued onto the shores of Australia. But a large majority did stay on in Waipu and made their home there, bringing up their families in the New

World.

The town only has a population of around 1,500, but it still has a very strong Scottish heritage. There are monuments around town commemorating the Scottish families who lived here, and the fallen heroes of the First World War.

A visit to the little museum in the town isn't expensive and is great for a little bit of nostalgia. You can search through the ancestry records and explore family trees; you might even find a long-lost cousin willing to give you a bed for the night.

Waiheke Island

Back closer to Auckland again, is Waiheke Island, which is a great place for walking, cycling, swimming or just chilling out. You get a ferry (frequent sailings) to the island from Auckland, and it only takes around 45 minutes.

Piha

Only forty minutes from Auckland, this place is great for a Sunday picnic, along an unusual beach, with black sand. The beach is a surfers' paradise, but I preferred just watching the spray rising and the waves crashing along the dark sand. You can climb the giant rock in the middle of Piha beach and look out to the Tasman Sea.

Karangahake

There are so many interesting and beautiful places to visit in New Zealand, it's difficult to choose where to go. I decided it was time for a bit of history, so travelled east from Auckland towards the Karangahake Gorge region. Aside from its rugged beauty, it also gives you a glimpse of New Zealand's gold mining history. The walking trails are fabulous, taking you along winding paths and into old dark tunnels with water dripping from the roof. Thank goodness for the torch on my phone. Guess what? In these remote tunnels, you can see glow worms, lit up in the dark. Careful on the slippery paths though, as you don't want to drop the hundreds of feet onto the rocky riverbanks below. Dangerous, but what an experience.

The Cathedral Cove (known as The Cove) is an awesome place. How nature carved out the beautiful designs on these giant rocks is unbelievable. You can see what I mean from my photograph.

Now, this was one place that I couldn't leave without having a swim. The waters were cold and the high waves washed me back onto the white sandy shores more than once. Being an old romantic, even though I was a solo traveller, I did think that this would be a perfect place for a proposal …

Then onto Mercury Bay, further along the eastern coast of the Coromondel Peninsula. Named by the English navigator James Cook. I was most intrigued by the visitors to the beach, rushing along to find where hot water bubbles through the golden sand. If you lie down on the beach, you can feel the heat seeping up through the sands. In some parts of the beach it's too hot to walk in bare feet. Why is the beach so hot? Well, underneath are hot water thermal springs. Very unusual, but another wonder of New Zealand.

Lots of Lovely Little Places

Paihia – This town is known as the gateway to the Bay of Islands. Beautiful scenery looking out to the islands, with the added attraction of dolphins near the shore. If you like fishing, then you might be lucky and catch a tasty snapper. A must-see in Paihia is the Haruru Falls, where I nearly … you guessed it … fell.

Kerikeri – A small town, but a favourite with tourists. Visit Puketi Rainforest and you will see kauri trees, which grow to an amazing 50 metres, that's over 160 feet tall. They also have a massive circumference, so if you fancy a tree hug, you might need to bring a friend or two. The trees can live for over 2,000 years, and no wonder, breathing in the freshness of the forest really is a tonic to the lungs.

Whangaroa Harbour – I was told a creepy tale here and one that goes back to the 1800s. Apparently, a New Zealand chief was so angry when his 10 year old son was insulted and laughed at by a group of Europeans who had just landed, that he sought revenge. Now, not only were around 70 people killed by the chief and his tribe, they were also eaten. Oh well, I suppose there wasn't much food around.

90 Mile Island – If you continue on the north-western coastline, you reach a place called 90 Mile Beach. The sand here is hard enough that you can drive for miles along the beach (only when the tide is out, mind, unless you're on a suicide mission). There are also giant dunes which have built up over hundreds of years, where visitors come to sand board. Great fun for everyone, though trekking up the dunes plays havoc with your calves.

Cape Reinga – You can't get any further north in New Zealand than Cape Reinga. This is a very special place in the hearts of the Maoris. This is their most sacred area, and they believe that when their souls leave their bodies after death, they come here to their eternal home. I can see why their souls have chosen this beautiful place, where the Tasman Sea meets the Pacific Ocean and they join together. It really is something else.

Waikato Region

Hamilton – A great place for a stopover as there are some great pubs and clubs in Hamilton. I was fortunate enough to choose a nice refreshment area where a jazz band was playing – wow, do I enjoy the sound of the saxophone. So, I sat back and relaxed with an ice cool cocktail to match the ice cool jazz.

Matamata – The drive through the farming country is made more interesting by all the horses you will see. No wonder, this area is famous for breeding and training thoroughbreds.

Hobbiton

My next destination was the lush pastures of Hobbiton, or The Shire from *Lord of the Rings*. You can journey through this magical land, on rough terrain through the mighty Kaimai Ranges (which means *beautiful mountains*). These mountains feature in a lot of Maori folklore, and as they tower above you, you can see why.

But most people are not here for the Maori tales, but to see the incredible setting of the *Lord of the Rings* trilogy. An aide or tour operator will show you around, pointing out the more famous locations and explaining how the movie was made.

One of the facts I heard, was that a man-made pond was dug to make the Shire look more authentic. They obviously did a good job, because the next thing, the pond was taken over by hundreds and hundreds of frogs. The bull frogs were so noisy trying to lure the females to mate, that it became impossible for the sound engineers to record the dialogue. They ended up having to catch all the frogs and relocate them to another pond, well away from the film set.

Did you know that the Orbs in the film were actually soldiers from the New Zealand army?

And also did you know that over 1,000 hobbit feet were made for the film?

Artificial trees were brought in to dress the set, but one of them wasn't the right colour, so every leaf on the giant tree had to be re-painted by hand. This required, not just a lot of patience, but a construction crane to lower the artists onto the tree.

After all the scenes were shot and the gates of the cameras have been checked, the director calls it a wrap. This phrase, usually heard in TV and film circles, means that the film has been completed or. At least, it's the end of the filming. It is then time to dismantle the set. But film buffs can still visit, and see where the Shires became a reality. In fact, today, this area is one of the biggest tourist attractions in New Zealand.

Next time I bump into my old pal, Billy Boyd (Pippin, the hobbit), from *Lord of The Rings*, I can tell him I've visited where he shot some of his scenes.

This was a truly wonderful experience and one that I will carry in my heart. I had not just visited Hobbiton, but also travelled into another world – Middle

ROGER CLIFFORD

Earth.

AUSTRALIA: ROGER THE DODGER DOWN UNDER

Sydney

Sydney is a vibrant city, with sky-high office blocks and thriving businesses. It is also one of the most beautiful cities in the world.

Here are some of the facts I unearthed while I was there. The city centre is built over a burial ground (I did say I unearthed the facts, didn't I?) but don't worry, that was over 200 years ago, and St. Andrew's Church now stands firmly on the spot.

Below the Queen Victoria Building are underground tunnels. They were never completed though, as the Sydney Bridge was built to help workers commute in and out of the city.

The bridge was built between 1923 and 1932 and was nicknamed The Iron Lung, as it breathed new life into the city. Others, who didn't view it as favourably, called it The Ugly Coat Hanger. It is recorded that 16 people lost their lives during the construction. Nowadays, you can climb to the top of the bridge, but only if you are wearing a harness, in case you lose your balance ... ahh.

Now, there's a funny wee story about the opening of the bridge in 1933. The Premier of New South Wales, Jack Lang, was there in his finery, to cut the ribbon and formally open the bridge. But then a guy called Francis Edward De Groot, galloped up on his horse and, like a true knight, drew his sword and with a swish, cut the ribbon. De Groot was a member of the new guard of Australia, which was a short-lived Australian monarchist and fascist organisation, which had sprung from the old guard. The new guard thought that the bridge should be opened by a respectable member the population (not a politician). Maybe he had a point.

There used to be a toilet under the bridge that didn't have a roof, but once they opened the bridge to walking groups, there were too many people stopping to have a look at the person spending a penny. Personally, I think there are much nicer things to look at in Sydney.

I was very fortunate whilst sightseeing at Sydney Harbour to witness a couple of Aborigines dressed in their ancestral costumes, necklaces, beads and body paint. Yip they were wearing the lot and blowing into their didgeridoos. These very large wind instruments make quite unusual noises and are best enjoyed when you've got a few glasses of wine down you. But I enjoyed the whole spectacle and offered some money to get my photo taken with them.

Another feature on the Harbour's skyline, is Sydney Tower (now Westfield Tower). Built between 1975 and 1981, it cost AU$36 million. In 2010 the Westfield Company refurbished the tower at a staggering cost of $1 billion. There's an observation gallery and a revolving restaurant (I told you there would be more than one). Again, I was treated to a nice meal as I went round and round, I got some spectacular views of the city at night, and snapped away happily with my camera.

A magnificent piece of architectural genius can be seen at St Mary's Church. It was built in 1821 and has a large Irish/Australian congregation. It is a stunning building and attracts a lot of tourists.

You'll know by now that I like a good park, and Hyde Park in Sydney is a good park. It takes its name from the London park, but unlike its English equivalent, it used to hold regular camel races. Some of the trees here are over 100 years old and are worth a visit and a hug.

By 1792, Britain had sent so many convicts to Australia that they represented 75% of the population. Most liked the country so much that even when their sentences were over, they decided to stay – well, it was either that or facing the sea-voyage home again.

In 2014 terror came to the streets of Sydney, with the Martin Place Siege where two people were killed by a gunman, Man Haron Monis. An artwork, *Reflection* by Jess Dare, now commemorates this event, with handcrafted flowers entombed in the pavement.

Another public artwork worth a visit is *Forgotten Songs* by Michael Thomas Hill. In the heart of the city centre, there are bird cages overhead playing the recorded songs of many different species of birds, including the Jackie Winter and Tawney Frogmouth (cracking names). Believe you me, it's really enjoyable sipping on your tea while the birds serenade you.

Sydney Opera House

The Sydney Opera House is by far the most famous in the world. Its distinctive design is meant to be an image of unfurled sails, although some people think that it looks like giant seashells. With over 40 shows most weeks, there is something for every taste. I had the opportunity to have a look around, and as you can imagine, the security is tight at this iconic building.

The structure of the building looks impossible to climb, but some people have tried, and have ended up being removed by the police for their troubles. A chap by the name of Paul Robeson, was the first person to perform at Sydney Opera House. In 1960, he climbed the steep scaffolding and sang Ol' Man River to the highly amused construction workers as they ate their lunch.

If you fancy moving to Sydney, you could look at the oldest surviving house. Built in 1815 it stands in Secular Square. Alternatively, you could buy a flat with a view of the Opera House for a cool AU$7 million. A one bedroom flat, would cost you approximately AU$1.5 million, rising to about AU$3.5 million for a two apartment, and wait for it … roughly an eye watering AU$6.5 million for a three apartment. Well if you've got it, it's a great view, when you draw your curtains open in the morning.

A miniature scale model of Sydney can be viewed in the Custom House, looking down through a glass floor. Very unusual, but highly impressive.

If you just want to stay a couple of nights, there is a hotel built on the site of the hanging area. For some reason the management don't like talking about this fun fact.

The Rock area of the city is famous for being the location of a notorious bank robbery. AU$1.7 million were stolen in 1978, a huge amount of money even now. The gang supposedly tunnelled under the bank and to this day the money has never been recovered. Some experts believe the stash is buried deep under the rocks of Circular Square, so if you have a shovel handy …

If you need a wee drink after all your digging, there is an Irish pub called the Hero of Waterloo, which dates back to 1843. It was said that back in those times, the staff would frequently add a little potion to the young men's ale. The secret potion made them drunk and incapable, so they would be carried down to the cellar where kidnappers would be waiting. Next thing they knew, they would be on small rowing boats heading for slavery on the larger boats that plied their trade in the southern seas. It might have been a nice wee earner for the staff at the pub, but it was a shocking hangover for the poor unfortunate who would wake up from their drunken slumber, far out at sea.

When I was very young, my mother and father, contemplated immigrating to Australia, as it was the land of opportunity. It certainly would have been a beautiful country to start out in. I was told later that my mother was all for it, but my father had work in Scotland, which was difficult to come by at that time. As it happens, we never emigrated. I'm glad that we stayed on in Scotland, *The Land of the Brave.*

Melbourne

Melbourne is the capital of the state of Victoria, with Federation Square at its centre. You'll find plenty of bars and restaurants here, and along the River Yarra. Melbourne was much cooler than Sydney, but still warm enough to get burned if you go out without the old suntan lotion on.

Did you know that Melbourne was founded by Batman? No joke. Okay, so it wasn't Batman and Robin, Batman, but an explorer and entrepreneur called John Batman. While he had British nationality, he was born in Tasmania. It was said that he negotiated with the local Aborigines to acquire the land, but what really happened remains a bit of a mystery, and the subject of debate. But regardless of how it was founded, the population grew steadily as more Tasmanian farmers followed Batman to Melbourne.

And how did Melbourne get its name? Well, it was named after the British Prime Minister William Lamb, 2nd Viscount of Melbourne Hall.

Another famous figure is the outlaw Ned Kelly, who is well-respected here in Melbourne and throughout Australia. Ned was of Irish heritage; his parents having come from Tipperary (not by choice, his father Red, was a transported convict). During his career in crime, Ned battled in a shoot-out with the police and killed three of them and so, he became the most wanted man in Australian history.

Eventually, after another gun battle that saw his brothers and fellow gang members killed, Kelly was arrested. He was found guilty and was sentenced to hang. Before his hanging in November 1880, he was asked for his final words and said, 'Such is life,' a phrase that is still well-used by Australians to this day.

I JUST WENT OUT FOR BREAD AND MILK

The iron suit that Ned Kelly wore as body armour can be seen in the State Library in Melbourne. Rumour has it that he told Judge Redmond Barry that it wouldn't be too long before they met again, on the other side. The judge died just two weeks after Kelly's execution. Coincidence or curse? You make up your own mind.

Did you know that Melbourne had a goldrush in 1851 that was even bigger than the one in California in 1880? Or that Mandarin is the second most commonly spoken language in Melbourne?

Another interesting fact I stumbled across was when I was in the Bourke Hill area, which contains the city's red-light district. It is said that there used to be a tunnel that linked the area with Parliament House. You can dig into that rumour, if you fancy a challenge. Personally, I would think that the politicians have more on their minds!?

Okay, let's move on and go down some of Melbourne's 260 alleyways. Great for exploring and you will be rewarded with some really beautiful little gems in the way of cafes, bistros, wine bars and restaurants. It was a great way to pass a Sunday, and I enjoyed a meal here, polished off with a bottle of local wine – Pinot Noir or Pinot Grigio – no, not both of them, well, if you insist.

One of the great things about Melbourne is the free tram system, which helped me get around. I loved my wander down Stevenson Lane to see street art, and then onto Federation Square which has a large cultural precinct. I enjoyed a couple of open-air shows there, and if you happen to visit one day, you might be lucky enough to catch a world-class event from its programme.

You'll also find the lavish Hamer Hall here, with its 2500-seat concert hall. I didn't get to a show, but I did have a sneaky look inside the magnificent building. On the outside is a huge spire, which looked to me like a poor man's Eiffel Tower. Moving down the street from Hamer Hall and onto Federation Square where you will find Flinders Train Station. Over 110,000 people commute through the station every day, on over 1,500 trains. If you're meeting a date there for the first time, you might need to do something special to stand out from the crowd.

You'll have gathered by now that while I am afraid of heights, I don't let it stop me, so up I went to the Eureka Skydeck in Melbourne which is literally out-of-this-world. Not only does the giant skyscraper pierce the clouds, but the lift takes you to the observation deck on the 88th floor in 38 seconds.

There is an extension that juts out of the side of the building made of toughened glass. It can take 12 people at a time, so if you feel brave enough, you might want to give it a go. But when you look down and see a Lego-sized city below your feet ... you might not feel quite so brave. Just to add to the tension, as you look down, there are cameras flashing from all directions to. At first you might think that there is a problem with the electrics, and if there's a problem with the electrics ... but don't worry, it adds to the excitement and you've a range of souvenir photos to choose from at the end – each one showing a *What the hell am I doing here?* expression on your face.

Adelaide

I flew into Adelaide, which is South Australia's coastal capital, and found it to be a great deal warmer than Melbourne. I stayed in lodgings close to Victoria Square, which was named in 1837 after the then Princess Victoria.

Adelaide's town hall (built in 1862) on William Street is a landmark for a variety of reasons. Queen Elizabeth visited it in 1954, and then in 1964, 300,000 cheering fans waved to the Beatles, who appeared on the balcony. Then in 1986 Pope John Paul II lit a candle for peace on the same balcony.

Edmund Wright, the architect and former mayor of the town had six faces carved in the keystones of the upstairs windows – two were Queen Victoria, one was Prince Albert, the others? Well, the architect never told anyone whose images they were, and it remains a mystery to this day.

There are many buildings in Adelaide which were built in the architecture of the Victorian era. One of the most striking is the Adelaide Arcade, which was the first building in the city to have electric lighting. The basement below the arcade used to house tearooms, but these are no longer used. You can take photos of them though, through a glass floor above the stairs to the tearooms. At the foot of the stairs there is a skeleton! It is said to commemorate the ghostly figure who has been seen many times around the arcade. It is thought to be Francis Cluney who was the caretaker there until his head was mutilated in the electricity generator. Yikes. Watch out, I'm going to get you …

The arcade leads onto one of Adelaide's busiest shopping streets – Rundle Mall – where you can also see some public art. There are four life-size, charismatic bronze pigs, who look like they are having a great day out at the Mall, in fact the sculpture is called *A Day Out*. They were designed by Marguerite Derricourt and are named Oliver (standing), Horatio (sitting), Snuffles (sniffing out a bargain) and little Augusta – aww.

The next piece you come across are two very large steel spheres, one on top of the other, which has become an Adelaide icon. Their name, well, *The Mall's Balls*. There doesn't seem to have been much thought put into naming those two, does there?

The Myre Centre, which is the second most expensive building in Adelaide, is situated in the Rundle Mall. Until a few years ago, it housed a rooftop theme park – Dazzleland – which holds treasured memories for a generation of South Australians.

Haigh's Chocolates, a famous Australian brand, can also be found, bought and eaten in Rundle Mall. During the annual Vogue festival, you can taste this delicious, though expensive, chocolate for free. Keep some dark chocolate for me, please.

If beer is more to your taste, then you'll also find Coopers Brewery here in Adelaide, which is the largest Australian-owned brewery. In 2003 they sold 69 million litres of beer. I must admit that I did enjoy a few glasses of the fine amber nectar, but 69 million litres, that's a lot of thirsty Aussies.

While Adelaide is now a vibrant city, a few years back, you would have called it conservative. So, what did they do to change? Well, they started by adopting a more Melbourne way of life, modernising along the way. Today it has an array of coffee shops, restaurants and bars around the city. Hic hic.

After all that sightseeing, it was time for a bit of unwinding, so I headed for Henley Beach. With sweltering sun, perfect swimming water and miles of white sand, what's not to love. I walked from the pier at one end of the beach and along the long stretch, and though I had slip, slapped and slopped, I still had a wee sun-glow by the end of the evening.

Cuddle Creek was also a great place to visit. With a name like that, you'd think it would be the ideal place for romance. Well, it is, but just for the wildlife and exotic animals. It's located in the Adelaide Hills to the south and there are loads of amazing species to see. But this is nothing like a zoo – it's much more open. It would be a great place to bring kids, but I loved it too. A kangaroo with a joey in her pouch took a very close interest in me, or maybe it was just my camera.

Another funny story which happened in Cuddle Creek was that I saw two rather wild looking dogs, in fact you might say they were barking mad. Well, then I heard a softer bark, which sounded like it was coming from above. Woof, woof. I looked up, and there in a tree was a large bird imitating the dogs. I later discovered that it was a barking owl. It made me laugh and really made my day.

During extremely hot weather Cuddle Creek is plagued by bush fires and sometimes rockslides which can disrupt public transport. But what the hell – live dangerously and tell the tales.

Brisbane

Brisbane is the capital of Queensland and was built around the Brisbane River. Interesting to a Scot like me, is that the city used to be called Edinglassie, after Edinburgh and Glasgow. It's the third most populous city in Australia, after Sydney and Melbourne, with a population of around 2.4 million.

Like many places in Australia, the biggest migration was due to transportation, and in 1788 around 162,000 criminals were shipped over. At one time, the convicts were paid in alcohol, just what you need to keep the peace.

By 1823 Brisbane was a small city and it needed a town hall. It had to wait until 1930 for the current one to be built and that was after they drained the swampland they wanted to build on.

If you take a trip to Observatory Park, you will get a glimpse of the dark, harsh history of the work the prisoners had to do. You can still see the Old Windmill which the convicts built and then ground corn. They worked long hours with little to eat or drink. And it wasn't just men who were shipped to Brisbane, there were a lot of violent females transported too. Those who reoffended were imprisoned at Eagle Farm, which is now an industrial suburb.

Not wanting to be left behind by the cities in the south, Brisbane had its very own goldrush in 1846.

The Black Plague hit Brisbane in 1920 and continued to kill people until it was eradicated about nine years later. It was thought that migrants carried the plague in on ships coming into the Brisbane ports.

In 1942 there was a full-scale battle on the streets of the city between US military personnel and Australian servicemen and civilians. It took place on the 26th and 27th of November. Tensions arose due to various factors, including the fact that the American military received more rations than their Australian counterparts which made them more of a hit with the ladies. So, the inevitable happened. By the end of the battle one Australian was killed and hundreds of people were injured. The American press were told to keep the brawl hushed up, so it was never reported in the US.

More saintly than the soldiers, was Mary Mackillop, who was canonised and became Brisbane's very own saint. Born of Scottish descent in Melbourne, you can see her statue in St Stephen's Chapel, the oldest church in Queensland, which sits next to the

I JUST WENT OUT FOR BREAD AND MILK

much larger St Stephen's Cathedral.

If you venture into the city's botanical gardens you can see the Clifton Cannon, sitting above the riverbank. This cannon was used by Wellington at the battle of Waterloo, having been manufactured in Falkirk, Scotland. You can also see Bunya Pine trees, which are sacred to the Australian Aborigines. The trees shed cones that can weigh about 10kg, so it could have serious consequences if it landed on your nut. Do you get it? Nut on nut. Oh, suit yourselves.

Walking along Queen Street, you can see thousands of decorative butterflies on the Wintergarden building at the Mall. They are lit up at night, making them even more beautiful.

One of the nicest places I visited in Brisbane was the South Bank, with its very own man-made beach. This is a paradise for adults and children alike. Get plenty of sun cream on though, as the sun is really strong. You might like to get a better view of the area by having a whirl on the big wheel, though you do need to keep your eyes open. At night the city is one of the most colourful I've ever seen.

The Gold Coast is only about an hour south of Brisbane and with its clear blue waters and white foam waves, it is certainly worth a visit. I walked the golden sands, starting at Broadbeach until it was time for a beer, or as the Aussies would say 'It's time for an ice-cold bottle of the old golden nectar matey and Gid day.' Well, something like that.

A strange thing to see in all this heat was Christmas lights. I even saw Santa walking about. Somehow, it just doesn't seem right in the sunshine.

Back to Sydney

There were two places I really wanted to visit before I flew out of Australia on further adventures. The first was Bondi Beach. This is one of the most beautiful beaches in the world, and I am not the only holiday maker who has it on their 'must see' list, in fact on a busy day it can attract over 40,000 people. The beach is just to the east of Sydney and has been featured in many TV programmes and movies. The first thing that catches your eye when you go onto the golden sands are the hourglass figures of the girls in small bikinis and the 6ft-something blonde haired guys with toned physic, all carrying surfboards. But this place isn't just about looking at the scenery, with the waves rising high and crashing onto the shore, it has a dangerous side to it too.

Lurking in the blue waters are dangerous currents and you should read carefully the safety notices put up by the lifeguards as to where the designated swimming areas are. It's not just the currents you need to look out for, these are also shark-infested waters. Every year surfers who ignore the warnings are attacked or even killed by sharks.

I had a lovely time, though, paddling along the edge of the water, ice cream in hand, when suddenly, it appeared from nowhere. No, don't worry, it wasn't a shark, but it was a sneaky wave that came in so quickly that it unbalanced me. My sunglasses were knocked off my face by it, and just as quickly as the wave came, it was gone, my sunglasses with it. I was left licking what was left of my ice cream and feeling a tiny bit guilty about my involuntary littering.

The second place I knew I needed to see were the Blue Mountains and the Three Sisters peak. I woke very early and after a good long brisk walk, I arrived at Sydney's Central Railway Station. After about a two-hour journey on a double-decker train, I got off at a little town called Wentworth. From there you can take a coach to the Blue Mountains, or do what I did, and walk along the Charles Darwin Walk, which takes you from Wentworth, through Jamieson Creek, to the top of Wentworth Falls.

The walk is about 2.5km long, and if you want to connect with nature, this is for you. There is a winding, rambling pathway resplendent with silver trees, sandbanks, bubbling streams and exotic birds, that you can see and hear on the overhead branches. You do need to be careful though, as there are no safety barriers and some parts are quite steep. It really was a tonic for the lungs though, with the pure forest air.

When you arrive at the viewpoint you won't be disappointed – you couldn't be – as before you stand the Blue Mountains. Are they really blue? I hear you ask. Well, the secret to their colour lies in the oil which comes from the numerous eucalyptus trees. The droplets of oil they secrete combine with the atmosphere and scatter blue light across the mountains. It is an absolutely stunning sight.

Travelling further west, I came to a town called Katoomba, famous for the Three Sisters. The Sisters are an unusual rock formation formed from land erosion over thousands of years, as the cliffs in the surrounding Jamieson Valley are slowly broken.

The Sisters are called Meehni, Wimlah and Gunnedoo. Aboriginal legend has it that the three beautiful sisters had fallen in love with three brothers from the Nepean tribe, but as marriage between the tribes was forbidden, an elder turned the women to stone. What happened to the brothers? Don't know, I haven't found them yet.

I have to mention that on my return to Sydney, I met a beautiful girl called Charlotte We met at the hostel where we were both staying. She was tall and very slim. She was also very good looking. What drew me to this lady was that she sat quietly, reading a book and looked a bit lonely. I asked if I could join her, she laughed and agreed. As we talked, she told me to keep talking, because she loved my Scottish accent. (Incidentally this was not the first time on my travels that I had been told, by others that they liked listening to the Scottish accent. Anyway, I told her that she had a great figure, and she told me that she used to be a ballerina when she was younger. She also told me that her grandmother who was now deceased had come from Dumfries, many years ago and settled in Perth, Australia which is where she was from. We drank Pinot Grigio into the late evening. Indeed, I had to make a few trips to the supermarket directly across the street to top up with another bottle or two. Eventually we made our way the TV room, where there was no one in the room due to the fact that there was some boring film playing that no one wanted to see. It was so natural that we kissed, all alone in the darkness of that room, with only our faces illuminated by the brightness of the screen. The hours passed quickly, and in the morning, she was gone. As I packed to make my way to the airport, I felt a little heartbroken. But now it was time to say goodbye to Australia and continue on my worldwide journey.

THAILAND

Bangkok

Since arriving in Bangkok, I have discovered it is a beautiful city of outstanding contrasts, where you have modern skyscrapers next to old buildings; and ancient temples are hidden in modern streets, giving you just a tantalising peak to know they are there.

Bangkok was established over 500 years ago on the banks of the Chao Phraya River and soon great palaces and temples sprang up. While foreigners know it as Bangkok, to the Thai people, it is the City of Angels (the second one of those I've visited in the past few months). Now there are over 8.5 million people in Bangkok and around 69 million in Thailand.

The oldest house in the city is the House on Sathon, or the Sathon Mansion, which is 128 years old. I think I can vaguely remember it being built.

The tallest skyscraper in Thailand, opened in 2016, is the King Power MahaNakhon, which has 77-storeys. (It had its title taken in 2018 by the Magnolias Waterfront Residences.)

But an eerie skyscraper can be found in the Sathon District. While it should have amazing views over the Chao Phraya river, there are few occupants to see them. While it was under construction the country's currency (the Baht) collapsed. The financial crisis throughout Asia in 1997 meant that there was no one to take ownership and the magnificent ghost building was left to rot. It is now home to drug addicts and vagrants.

The 47-storey tower is officially called the Sathon Unique (ironic), but the locals call it the Ghost Tower. It is said that the building is haunted by the ghost of a Swedish backpacker who was found hanging on the 43rd floor. Personally, I'm more afraid of the live residents.

One of the things you really notice about Bangkok is how busy it is, and nowhere is busier than the Chong Nonsi junction which has around 50,000 people travelling through it every day. As you can imagine, there are some really heavy traffic jams here. I witnessed one, sitting in a taxi. I was glad I wasn't a pedestrian that day as the traffic keeps coming, even when the little green man is on. Quick run!

If you ever get a chance to visit Thailand, you will fall in love with it. The people are the nicest, friendliest, most helpful people I have ever met. It was a joy staying in Bangkok, but now it's time to go further afield.

Koh Samui

After a couple of flights, I landed in Koh Samui where I was due to meet up with my son and some of his friends. Little did I know that they had also arranged for a very good friend of mine, Kev, to

I JUST WENT OUT FOR BREAD AND MILK

meet up with us too. Kev had just finished acting in a small film called Mara: The seal Wife. Inspired by Celtic folklore.

Koh Samui is the second largest island in Thailand with amazing golden beaches and evergreen forests. You'll not miss the island's magnificent golden Buddha, which sits on a small rocky island. You can walk up the stairway, which has a beautiful colourful dragon design, to the platform on which the big Buddha sits nearly 40 ft high. It is visible by air when you land on the island.

I stayed in the Chaweng area which is the busiest town in Koh Samui, and it is tourism that keeps the town afloat. The nightlife is fantastic, but before you get the wrong idea, it was Thai boxing that kept me entertained that night, though I didn't agree with all of the refereeing decisions.

The next morning came quickly, and we were driven about an hour out of town where the Ultimate Challenge awaited. We hand-glided through the forest, then travelled down a waterchute, next to a waterfall, at 90 miles per hour. When you hit the pool at the bottom, you think you might never emerge from it. My ribs are still sore.

Then it was time for my son and his friends to return to the UK. My friend Kev and I travelling on to Koh Phangan.

Koh Phangan

I took a ferry to the island of Koh Phangan, about an hour from Koh Samui, landing at the small port town of Thong Sala, before moving further along the coastline to the town of Haad Rin. This town hosts famous Full Moon Parties which attract up to 30,000 locals and tourists alike. Unfortunately, the town was extremely quiet. Kev, and I tried out some of the local beers, and cocktails. I

won't be here for the next one on the 22nd of December. Pity, but never mind, ho ho ho, at least Santa is coming.

During one particular evening, on the beach I met a lovely lady. I know what you might think 'A Thai lady, oh aye?' but actually it wasn't. This lady came from London, her name was Emily. We drank wine, which we both enjoyed. And we got on very well. She had been with other friends, but we broke away to a little quieter area of the beach. We swapped stories, of where we had been and things that we had seen on our travels. As the night wore on, we did have an intimate kiss and cuddle, as the moonbeams danced across the frothy waves. P.S. It was a bit spicier than that that, but that's a story for another book.

Phuket

I JUST WENT OUT FOR BREAD AND MILK

After a few days on the island, it was time to explore some of the other islands. I left Koh Phangan, and after a short journey on the ferry, and believe you me, these Islands have ferries to take you anywhere, I arrived on the island of Phuket in what can only be described as roasting weather.

Travelling a good hour from the airport, I arrived in Phatong, where I was met with an array of nightclubs, restaurants and bars. There is a nice beach too, Patong, for the sun worshipers. But if nightlife is what you are after, you won't be disappointed, as the place really gets going about 7pm and you can party until 3am or later. Don't worry if you need a hangover cure, as nearly every shop sells alcohol.

On a day out when I was on the island, I had the chance to take in some great sight-seeing places:

- Another Big Buddha: A splendid masterpiece, which stands 147 feet (45 metres) high. Built high on the mountain: it is a landmark on the island.
- Kata Viewpoint: Has great views over Kati Noi Beach

and is always busy throughout the year.

- Chalong Temple: This holy temple is the most important temple in Phuket. The inside is beautiful: the walls decorated with beautiful paintings. As always shoes must be removed when you go inside the temple.

- The Honey Market: This visit was really fascinating. The Market is a farm shop, which not only sells an assortment of honey products but staff are on hand to tell you all the benefits of eating honey. You also get a chance to watch the busy bees working away in their hives.

- Visiting the Elephants: I had the chance to come close to the elephants and even stroke their trunks. They are very friendly and like visitors making a fuss over them. The owners will charge a very small fee, if you want your photo taken with one. One thing I wanted to find out, and was reassured to hear, was that the elephants are well looked after.

- Karon (pronounced Karong) is a beautiful beach a little further round the coastline from Patong and is a much more family-friendly place. It was nice to come here to get away from some of the hustle and bustle … if you know what I mean. The water here is crystal clear and warm, if you fancy a swim. You can even order an ice shake on the beach, with many varieties to choose from. My preference was banana. The downside was that you sweat constantly in the soaring heat, so lots of sun cream and lots of drinks are a must.

Raya Island

Leaving from Sharon Pier (pronounced Sharong), I travelled to Raya Island, just south of Phuket, by speedboat. This was a fantastic experience. These boats travel at some speed and u can come straight off the water, only to come back down among the waves with a thud and a mouthful of spray, if you're not lucky. I wouldn't have changed it for the world. I felt that I was flying over the waters. Perhaps on a secret mission. Just to deliver Milk Tray, chocolates to the lady. Though I wouldn't fancy being the man in black in this heat.

The waters around Raya are a magnificent blue-green, and there are plenty of opportunities to take boat trips and dive into the cool water from the boat. I also had a chance to try some snorkelling here. It took a wee while to get used to breathing through the snorkel, but there was no better way to view the corals and tropical fish. The fish are a rainbow of different colours but watch out ... they will nibble on your fingers if you let them.

The food on the island was great, and really inexpensive. I finished off a great meal with fresh watermelon and pineapple. Lovely jubbly.

One of the great things about travelling is meeting the locals, and here the locals are giant Goanna lizards. The roam freely about the place, sauntering across roads and swimming in the island's pools. Watch out though, they have sharp teeth and claws.

I went from Raya by speedboat (I'm getting used to this lifestyle), to Coral Island, a place which lives up to its name – it is made from coral. The reefs are beautiful, but beware, there are spine sea urchins dotted about, which can be very painful if you step on one. So, keep to the designated areas of the beach, where it is perfectly safe to sunbathe and swim. I didn't go near the corals and stayed out of the water too, but I did manage an ice cool banana smoothie.

Phi Phi

Landing on the island of Phi Phi takes around two hours by ferry, and what a lovely trip it was, with the sun beating down on me. The island only has a population of around 3,000 but it became famous as the location for the film *The Beach*. I was lucky to see the amazing Maya Bay, as since I have returned, it has been closed to tourists to help it recover from its over-popularity.

The island was well-worth the visit though, with beach raves, cool beers and plenty of wild entertainment. It also has great places to snorkel in the blue waters off the coast. I would happily have stayed there and become a tanned beach bum, but I was being pulled to see more of what the world had to offer.

On a sadder note, the island was badly affected by the tsunami in 2004 with around 70% of buildings destroyed and anything between 850 and 4,000 people losing their lives.

James Bond Island

On this warm sunny morning, though every day is warm and sunny here, I travelled to the province of Phang Nga in southern Thailand. There I hopped on what can only be described as a motorised canoe, which took me through the Ao Phang Nga National Park. This was a beauty to behold with waterways and tall limestone islets (that's wee islands for those of you reaching for your dictionary right now).

After another short boat trip, I arrived on Khao Phing Kan, better known as James Bond Island. The island was used as the backdrop for some of the scenes in *Goldfinger*.

Today I was wearing:
- my short-sleeved tiger shirt
- my ultra-tight sexy shorts
- my Specsavers sunglasses
- my hair gelled back

Because today I was James Bond 007 - Licensed to thrill.

After a walk around, where I didn't spot any master criminals, I headed to the fishing village of Koh Pan-Yee for lunch. This floating village has a small market square, right in the middle of the sea, with other islets (I've already told you what they are) dotted around it.

Leaving this lovely place with my tummy full, it was back to land and onwards to visit the Monkey Cave at Wat Suwan Kuha Temple. Not only is this an underground Buddhist temple, it is also home to families of monkeys. I visited the temple and had my horoscope read (which sounded very promising) then fed the cheeky wee monkeys some fruit. They come down from the mountains and are very tame and friendly, at least to those who feed them. They have lovely soft hands. (I wonder if they thought the same about me?)

Then it was back to the Ao Nang Beach Resort, where I was staying. I would highly recommend Krabbi as an excellent place to visit as you are within easy reach of various islands (there are over 200 to choose from).

I've been in Thailand for nearly five weeks now but will definitely return if I can. It is a beautiful place to visit, and it is no wonder that tourism is one of its main industries. The day trips to the islands were all packed, but who could blame the tourists for wanting to see this amazing place.

SINGAPORE

After leaving the beauty of Thailand, my next destination was Singapore, with a population of five and a half million living in around 300 square miles.

Legend has it that Singapore was founded many centuries ago by a prince. When he landed on the island, he saw a lion and took it as a good omen, so he called the place Singapura, which means lion city.

Marina Bay is a must-see in Singapore, with its resort front and bars, restaurants and basically everything you could ask for. The street circuit around the Bay is the venue for the Singapore Grand Prix, which has 61 laps, but is also the slowest as it has so many twists and turns.

Then there is Merlion Park where you can see a statue of the mythical Merlion, which has the head of a lion and the body of a fish. The body symbolises Singapore's humble beginnings as a fishing village and the lion represents the city's original name.

The water-spouting statue stands at eight and a half metres tall and weighs 70 ton. It was unveiled by Prime Minister Lee Kuan Yew in 1972.

You just have to cross the Helix Bridge when you come to Singapore. It is a pedestrian bridge with a difference: its practical purpose is to link Marina South with Marina Bay; but it is designed to represent the double helix shape of DNA. The chemical bases of DNA, cytosine, guanine, adenine and thymine are represented in pairs of lights illuminating the letters, and in symbols embedded in the walkway.

Singapore's National Stadium is located in Kallang. It has a capacity of 55,000 and is well-used by football, rugby and cricket. Just as well, it cost two billion Singapore dollars to construct.

And now to Clifford Pier, I couldn't believe it. I was admiring an area of Collyer Quay at Marina Bay when I discovered Clifford Pier. It was named after a colonial governor of Singapore, Sir Hugh Clifford. That was a nice little touch to the end of the day. I must find out if we're related. You just never know! This guy Sir Hugh Clifford might have been a distant relative! I might even be a descendant from Royalty! There's not many Clifford's about? Well, there's no harm in dreaming.

MALAYSIA

Kuala Lumpur

And on I go … from Singapore to another vibrant and colourful city, Kuala Lumpur. The population of Malaysia is almost 32 million, with over 7 million in KL. Its currency is the Ringgit, and with a favourable exchange rate, I found the place great value for money.

Kuala Lumpur means muddy convergence (where rivers meet), but now it is home to amazing shopping. As I said, it's not too expensive, so it might be time for some Christmas shopping.

The city has 53 skyscrapers (I hope you're impressed: I was).

The Kuala Lumpur Tower was completed in 1995 and is the 7th tallest freestanding tower in the world. I should know, I've been up a few during my travels. The tower is made even more imposing by the fact that it was built on a hill.

It does have stiff competition from the Petronas Twin Towers, which have become iconic (they feature in the climax of the 1999 film *Entrapment*). These towers stand side by side – giant identical twins. They are officially the tallest twin buildings in the world, reaching up 88-storeys. I wouldn't like to have a room at the top and be told that the lift was out of order.

When I was standing taking a selfie of the Petronas Twin Towers, I texted one of my daughters, who after leaving school, studied as a professional dancer. I told her where I was, and to my surprise, she told me that whilst working on one of her cruise-line jobs, she and her friends, went sightseeing in Kuala Lumpur and actually made it to the top of The Petronas Towers.

But night was falling into darkness, and it was time to move on. I looked down at my feet and could see two big toes beginning to peek through the trainers I had bought six months previously in New York. I had to laugh to myself, and thought, 'Good job, there's no frost.'

I travelled around KL by monorail which runs high above the congested streets, out of the belching fumes and tooting horns. It's quick and reliable and an unusual way to travel.

Then it was time to head back across the border to Singapore, which involved a long wait as passengers had to disembark from their coaches and go through immigration individually.

SINGAPORE – DUBAI – LONDON – GLASGOW

And then, that was it. Suddenly, I was coming to the end of my adventures and it was time to go home to Scotland. I had planned to go on to the Philippians, but members of my family wanted me back home for Christmas. I hope you have enjoyed the fun as you travelled with me, across the many countries over the last six months. It's been quite remarkable how many people followed my exploits via social media, and encouraged me to put all my crazy, but informative, stories into a collection.

So, that's me heading back to Bonnie Scotland, where I can wander off to the shores of Loch Lomond at a moment's notice and be back in time for tea with family and friends in the evening. Phew. What an adventure.

PROCEEDS FROM MY BOOK

When I walked across all those countries, I also saw people who were homeless or rough sleepers for whatever reason. It's not for me to judge, but those poor people had nothing. Returning to Glasgow, Scotland it was no different. There are homeless people everywhere.

I can help a little, by giving the proceeds from the sale of my book to the homeless centres across Glasgow, Scotland, and all major cities in the world.

ACKNOWLEDGEMENT

Scotland – With Thanks

Since my oversea adventure, I have now returned to my native Scotland, and it was grand to have a lovely Christmas with family and friends. Now that my adventures are over for the present time, there are a few people who certainly helped along the way, to enjoy my journey. These are the people I would like to acknowledge. Firstly, I must point out that a lot of it wasn't intended or planned, it just sort of happened. I had been travelling for the past six months and returned with an abundance of knowledge and stories from all the places I had visited. I was also lucky that family and friends enriched my adventures. When I landed in New York, the birthplace of my father, my lovely niece Aisling McLaughlin and my great-nephew, Fergal, met me at John F. Kennedy Airport. And what a welcome it was with welcome balloons tied to the handle of the baby's buggy. Aishling drove me around the neighbourhoods of New York, as I took photos and collected stories. I salute you. I was pleasantly surprised by the arrival of my younger sister Marian, who flew from Ireland, and my one of my other nieces, who joined us from Abu Dhabi. We had a great time together, and visited Lady Liberty of the U.S. of A. I salute you. When I landed in San Francisco I was met at the airport by my good friend Bill Rogue who is an actor, performer and now-teacher in San Fran. Bill took me to his beautiful home in Silicon Valley where I met his lovely wife Fiona and their three fantastic children. To Bill and family: I salute you. As the weeks drifted by, I was bound onwards, and flew to the beautiful country of New Zealand, where I was met at Auckland airport by one of my beau-

tiful daughters Alison, and I met my little grandson of one year old for the first time, Griff Lewis-Clifford. I just had to give a big hug to this little toddler with blonde hair and lagoon blue eyes. My stay in New Zealand, and all the magical sights I visited around the island, was certainly helped by my daughter Alison, daughter-in-law Nic, and grandson Griff: I salute you During my stay in Auckland, I met up with an old friend from my neighbourhood in Clydebank, Jeff McKnight, and his lovely wife Carmen. My daughter and I were invited to their home for a beautiful meal. Imagine my surprise when Jeff invited me through to the garage, where I sat in his gleaming Rolls Royce. I can't thank you enough for your hospitality: I salute you. I also met a very famous couple through my daughter and Nic, whilst I was in New Zealand. The husband is world famous. He has made history!!! and has certainly put New Zealand on the map. I stayed over at one their holiday homes, on an island off Auckland. I also respect their privacy. Thank You: I salute you. When I flew to Australia and landed in Sydney, I met up with my son Roger Jnr's friend Joe Smith. A Clydebank boy, doing well in the business markets of Sydney. Joe took me to the Sydney skyscraper revolving restaurant for a meal. He also took me to vantage points overlooking the city as the sun set to capture fantastic photos. Joe Smith: I salute you. I travelled to Thailand where I met up with my son Roger and some of his friends. We all had a brilliant time: I salute you. I was certainly greatly surprised when my very good friend and actor Kev Kelly appeared in a bar on the beautiful island of Koh Samui. I knew I had been set up, but what I surprise I got. We all had a short, but great time. Kev stayed on for two weeks before flying back home. Kev: I salute you. When I landed in the beautiful city of Singapore, again I was fortunate enough to meet up with an old friend. We both studied engineering after leaving school. Joe Ferry now a senior engineer, in Thailand and Singapore. Joe took me around the night spots of the city, which was truly amazing, as we weaved our way through some of the top establishments. I salute you When I returned home to Scotland just a few days before Christmas, my youngest daughter Claire, flew from her home and busi-

ness in Lanzarote, to be with me for Christmas. Little did I know that all the family was going to be there. What a Christmas to come home to. What a Christmas we had. I salute you all.

ABOUT THE AUTHOR

Roger Clifford

Roger Clifford was born in Glasgow, Scotland, and lives in Clydebank, just outside Glasgow. He studied as an engineer, after leaving school. Then studied for a Bachelor of Art at The Royal Scottish Academy of Music and Drama, before taking up teaching in Glasgow. Roger is a teacher, actor and entrepreneur. He now hopes to pursue his work, through acting and writing.

Printed in Great Britain
by Amazon